THAI

COOKBOOK

70 Easy Recipes For Stir Fry Noodles Tom Yum
And Traditional Dishes From Thailand

Emma Yang

The trademarks that are used are without any consent, and the publication of the trademark is without permission or backing by the trademark owner. All trademarks and brands within this book are for clarifying purposes only and are the owned by the owners themselves, not affiliated with this document.

Contents

Introduction

Never despair if you have not figured out a way to go on an adventurous backpacking trip across Thailand. In the comfort of home, you can taste a true Thai experience worthy of your taste buds. There's no going back once you've discovered the flavors of Thai food.

Thai cuisine is well-known in the world. This one-of-a-kind cuisine is a fusion of East and West impacts dating back centuries. Harmony is an essential component of any dish. For Thai food to be genuine, the flavors and spices must be mixed cooperatively. The key characteristic of Thai cuisine is that each food should contain four basic flavors: sweet, spicy, salty, and sour. Chilies provide the heat, while sugar or fruit sugar provides the flavor. The alkalinity arises from star anise or lemon slices, whereas the salt concentration comes from sesame oil, shrimp paste, or fish sauce, among other things. Vegans can check with the diner to see whether any vegetable dishes include a fish sauce or seafood paste.

Various areas of Thailand and specific chefs can favor one of the four senses over the others, which is why a set of seasonings, such as salt, seafood or soy sauce, mustard, and dry or new chili, is often placed on the table in Thailand. As a result, the diner will change the balance to his or her preference. So, if you are served a meal that's still not really to your liking, such as one that's not hot enough, you can change the seasonings.

Savory, honey, sour, salty, and spice are the five main flavors in a typical Thai meal. Many Thai dishes are not considered complete unless they include all five. Although the seasoning may be hot for a western palate, Thai cuisine assures that all flavors are balanced.

A community of Thai diners will enjoy a handful of beef and fish dishes, as well as veggies, a pasta dish, and probably soup while dining out or preparing a meal at home.

Except for the soup, which each person can request, or each person receives a private bowl to receive a portion of the stew, everything is distributed. Fresh fruit, like mango or any of the hundreds of exotic fruits found throughout the world, can be served as a sweet. It may also be more creative, such as colorful rice cakes, tamarind chutney dumplings, fruit jelly, or a bean cake.

With these extinct flavors, "Thai Cookbook" has a wide range of delicious Thai recipes. It has five chapters with appetizers, snacks, breakfast, lunch, dinner, desserts, and Thai's most famous recipes. Read this book, follow these recipes, and have a flavorful, delicious meal every day.

Chapter 1: Introduction to Thai Cuisine

Food is an important part of every social gathering in Thailand, and it is often used as a social event or a reason to be happy. This is partly due to Thai people's pleasant, peaceful nature, but it's also simply because of how food is prepared, consumed, and enjoyed. Food brings people together and allows them to bond.

1.1 History of Thai Cuisine

The flavors of modern-day Thailand have their origins in ancient culture. The Thai people developed what is now known as the core of Siamese delicacies: different types of meat and fish coupled with rice, local veggies, spices, and aromatic citrus and chili as early as the 12th century. After, the Chinese brought pasta and the most popular Thai cooking weapon, the steel skillet, to Thailand.

Thai cuisine is strongly influenced by Traditional spices and flavors, as evidenced by the country's popular green, orange, and yellow curries. Thai curries are difficult to compare with Indian curries because they use several Indian spices in their seasonings while still retaining their distinct flavors thanks to locally sourced ingredients like Thai essential oils, rosemary, and galangal.

Other neighboring countries, such as Vietnam, Indonesia, Cambodia, Laos, Myanmar, and Malaysia, have influenced Thai cuisine. The nuanced flavor of modern Thai cooking—one of the fastest production and most famous cuisines—is the product of many diverse influences.

1.2 Traditional History of Thai Dishes

Thais avoided using large animals in large pieces because of their Buddhist heritage. Shredded large cuts of beef were seasoned with spices and herbs. Thai traditional recipes included stewing, cooking, and roasting. Roasting, stir-frying, and intense were all introduced as a result of Chinese trends. From the 17th and 18th centuries onwards, Dutch, Portuguese, English, and Japanese cuisines influenced the cuisine. Chilies were first exposed to Thai cuisine by Portuguese priests in the late 1600s, who had developed a taste for them while working in South America.

Rice is one of the most important ingredients in Thai cuisine. Rice is by far the most often served food at all dinners, and it is never discarded. Thailand produces and serves a wide range of rice cultivars, with Jasmine being the most common and the most costly. White rice is plentiful and less costly than Jasmine rice while being still tasty. Glutinous, or steamed rice, is also fairly popular, and brown bread is abundant and less costly than Jasmine rice while being still yummy. Another significant feature of Thai culture is the formal presentation of meals. The dining experience is influenced by attention to detail and how appealing it appears when served.

Irrespective of the delicious flavors, the dish must be visually pleasing, and this feature respects Thai culture's reverence for its food items. Even though the Chinese introduced utensils to Thailand many years ago, most Thais tend to use Western knives and forks in their unique way. A fork and a big spoon are the most popular pieces of Thai cutlery. The fork helps organize the foods on the spoon before taking it to the mouth, and the teaspoon is kept in the right wrist and is used in replacement of a knife. There is no need for a blade since all of the dishes are already sliced up.

1.3 Nutritional Information and Health Benefits of Thai Food

Thai cuisine is unquestionably good, but some of it can also be very nutritious. Eating foods containing these components has been linked to numerous medical benefits. Chili pepper is good for our lungs because it aids in the removal of coughing. It also has anti-inflammatory properties. Chilies and black peppercorns help enhance our digestive system's ability to digest food while also promoting digestive wellbeing. It prevents the formation of intestinal disorders, and the surface shell of the peppercorn also helps in the dissolution of fat cells. Ginger can be used to treat a variety of vomiting and gastrointestinal upsets. It contains a lot of gingerols, which have anti-inflammatory and antioxidant effects. Before being used in Thai dishes, ginger is typically diced or broken. Vitamin C, B Vitamins, and Manganese are all abundant in garlic. Garlic's chemical ingredients can help to lower blood stress (hypertension). It can aid in the reduction of cholesterol levels, potentially lowering the risk of cardiovascular disease. Many Thai dishes call for smashed, sliced, or even entire garlic cloves!

1.4 Key Ingredients to Prepare Thai Dishes at Home

Assemble these ten items, and you'll have everything you need to make Thai food at home.

- Shallots and Garlic

- Fresh Herbs

- Black Pepper

- Limes

- Thai Fish Sauce

- Rice

- Chiles

- Curry Paste

- Coconut Milk

- Vinegar

While Thai cuisine is renowned for its incredible combination of sour, sweet, salty, and crispy flavors, it is very simple to prepare at home. Gather these ten simple items, and you'll have everything you need to get started making Thai.

Chapter 2: Thai Breakfast and Snack Recipes

2.1 Thai Breakfast Omelets

Cooking Time: 30 minutes

Serving Size: 4

Ingredients:

- 1 cup bean sprouts
- ½ cup fresh coriander leaves
- 2 medium tomatoes
- 150g green beans
- 100g cup mushrooms
- 1 medium red capsicum
- 1 long red chili
- 1 ½ tablespoon vegetable oil
- 2 tablespoons lime juice
- 1 ½ tablespoons fish sauce
- 8 eggs

Method:

1. In a big jug, mix the eggs, lemon juice, shrimp paste, sugar, and chili.

2. In a large nonstick saucepan, heat two tablespoons of oil on moderate flame. Cook the mushroom and cabbage together.

3. Toss in the tomato. Cook for an additional minute, stirring occasionally, or until mildly softened.

4. Green beans should be put in a heatproof container in the meantime.

5. In a mixing bowl, mix the mushroom paste, peas, and artichokes.

6. Clean the pan with a damp cloth.

7. In a separate pan, heat one teaspoon of the cooking liquid over a moderate flame.

8. ¼ of the beaten egg should be poured into the bowl.

9. ¼ of the mushrooms solution should be spread over one-half of each omelet. To completely cover the filling, fold the paper over.

10. Serve with the remaining chili and cilantro.

2.2 Thai Breakfast Soup

Cooking Time: 50 minutes

Serving Size: 4

Ingredients:

- 3 teaspoons agave nectar
- ½ cup cilantro
- 1 can coconut milk
- 1 tablespoon fresh lime juice
- 1 large bunch of scallions
- ½ teaspoon kosher salt
- 1 tablespoon tamari
- 1 cup red lentils
- 2 cups vegetable broth
- 5 garlic cloves
- 3 medium plum tomatoes
- 4 tablespoons red curry paste
- 1½ pounds sweet potatoes
- 2 tablespoons ginger

Method:

1. Fill the Instant Pot halfway with vegetable broth.
2. Combine the green onion, cloves, ginger, potatoes, peppers, red curry paste, kidney beans, salt, tamari or soy sauces, and lite coconut milk in a large mixing bowl.
3. Choose a pressure level.

4. Set the pressure cooker to high and the cooking time to ten minutes.

5. Combine the lemon juice, agave or honey, and minced cilantro in a mixing bowl.

6. Taste the broth and season with salt and pepper as needed.

7. To eat, ladle soup into bowls and top with desired garnishes.

8. Hold leftovers refrigerated for up to 4-5 days.

2.3 Thai Chicken and Rice Soup

Cooking Time: 30 minutes

Serving Size: 6

Ingredients:

- 1 tablespoon lime zest
- 2 tablespoon cilantro
- 1 can coconut milk
- 2 tablespoon lime juice
- 2 tablespoon sugar
- 4 cups chicken broth
- 4 carrots
- 12 oz. chicken breasts
- 2 tablespoon Thai red curry paste
- 5 oz. shiitake mushrooms
- 1 medium red bell pepper

Method:

1. In a 6 quart Instant Pot, combine the vegetables, bell pepper, mushrooms, meat, curry paste, butter, and stock.

2. Preheat the pressure cooker to high pressure and set the timer for four minutes.

3. When you're done, press Cancel and release pressure using the fast release process.

4. Mix in the coconut milk after removing the chicken from the oven.

5. Return the shredded chicken to the oven.

6. Cook for an additional minute or until hot on the sauté level.

7. Just before eating, insert the lime zest and juice.

2.4 Thai Morning Glory Stir Fry

Cooking Time: 5 minutes

Serving Size: 4

Ingredients:

- ½ tablespoon oyster sauce
- 1 tablespoon vegetable oil
- ½ tablespoon soybean paste
- ½ tablespoon soy sauce
- 4 Thai hot chili
- 3 large cloves of garlic
- 1 bunch water morning glory

Method:

1. Put the morning glory in a container and break it into 4 inch long parts.
2. Then weigh the sauce ingredients and add them to the bowl as well.
3. Add the garlic and bell peppers to the edge of the dish, broken up.
4. In a large skillet, add the oil until it is very warm, then insert the container's components all at once.
5. Mix and fry rapidly till the morning glory is softened, having to turn for the lower part.

2.5 Golden Purses Thai Appetizer

Cooking Time: 30 minutes

Serving Size: 25

Ingredients:

- 1 cup bean sprouts
- ½ cup fresh coriander leaves
- 2 medium tomatoes
- 150g green beans
- 100g cup mushrooms
- 1 medium red capsicum
- 8 eggs
- 1 long red chili
- 1½ tablespoons vegetable oil
- 1½ tablespoons fish sauce
- 2 tablespoons lime juice

Method:

1. Combine shrimp, pork belly, mushrooms, onions, fresh basil, herb soy sauce, and garlic powder in a mixing bowl.
2. Using a teaspoon, scrape a spoon full of the paste onto the wrapping.
3. To make a little bag, push the sides up and pinch them together.
4. Repeat until you've used up half of the solution.
5. In a frying pan or skillet, heat the oil until it is very warm.
6. Fry once lightly browned, about 5 minutes. To drain natural oils, place them on a clean cloth.

7. Serve with a dipping sauce made from Thai sweet chilies.

2.6 Baked Thai Peanut Chicken Egg Rolls

Cooking Time: 18 minutes

Serving Size: 4

Ingredients:

- ¼ red bell pepper
- Nonstick cooking spray
- 1 medium carrot
- 3 green onions
- 2 cup rotisserie chicken
- ¼ cup Thai peanut sauce
- 4 egg roll wrappers

Method:

1. Preheat the air fryer to 390 degrees Fahrenheit.
2. Mix the chicken with the Thai chili sauce in a tiny bag.
3. On a clear, dry board, spread out the egg roll bags.
4. Organize ¼ of the carrot, red pepper, and vegetables over the lower quarter of an egg roll wrapping.
5. Half a cup of the chicken solution can be spooned over the veggies.
6. Use mist, dampen the wrapper's exterior surfaces.

7. Pull the wrapper's sides toward the middle and curl securely.

8. Put the egg rolls in the air fryer and cook for eight minutes until it is light golden brown.

9. Break in half and use more Thai Peanut Sauce on the side for stuffing.

2.7 Leaf Wrapped Snack

Cooking Time: 40 minutes

Serving Size: 4

Ingredients:

- 1 cup shallots
- ½ cup fresh coriander leaves
- 2 medium tomatoes
- 150g green beans
- 100g cup palm sugar
- 1 medium coconut
- 2 tablespoons lime juice
- 1 long red chili
- 1 tablespoon vegetable oil
- 1½ tablespoons fish sauce

Method:

1. To stop the fire, dry toast the almond in a skillet on moderately high, stirring frequently.

2. Strike the parsley and galangal together in such a rock mortar and pestle until perfect.

3. Add water, shrimp paste, oyster sauce, and shallot/galangal combination to a small casserole dish.

4. Lessen the sauces to the consistency shown in the image below by boiling them over moderate flame.

5. Take the cooked coconut from the flame and place it in a shallow saucepan.

2.8 Thai-Style Chicken Lettuce Wraps

Cooking Time: 40 minutes

Serving Size: 4

Ingredients:

For the Peanut Sauce

- ½ tablespoon ginger
- 1 clove garlic
- 1 tablespoon honey
- 1 tablespoon soy sauce
- ½ cup chicken broth
- ½ tablespoon Sriracha
- 2 tablespoon peanut butter

For the Chicken

- 4 lime wedges
- 8 iceberg lettuces
- Cooking spray
- 2 tablespoon peanuts
- Cilantro leaves
- 16 oz. ground chicken
- 2/3 cup scallions
- ¾ cup red cabbage
- 1 tablespoon Sriracha
- 1 tablespoon soy sauce
- ¾ cups carrots

- 1 tablespoon fresh ginger

- 4 cloves garlic

Method:

1. Mix chicken stock and half of the seasoning in a medium bowl and steam, stirring periodically, for five to six minutes over moderate flame.

2. In the meantime, fire a big nonstick skillet or broiler over a high, moderate flame until it is very hot.

3. Wait until the chicken is cooked through and golden brown, then add the garlic, sriracha, and spice and cook for another minute.

4. Heat for two minutes after adding the tablespoon of sour cream.

5. Sauté the sliced vegetables and ½ cup scallions until crispy and soft, around 1-2 minutes.

6. Serve with lemon wedges.

7. Split the chicken evenly among eight lettuce leaves, cover with shredded cabbage and leftover green onions.

8. Sprinkle with peanuts, peanut sauce, and coriander for garnish, and top with lemon wedges.

2.9 Yam Kai (Thai Eggs) with Leftover Grains

Cooking Time: 50 minutes

Serving Size: 2

Ingredients:

- 1 cup bean sprouts
- ½ cup fresh coriander leaves
- 2 medium tomatoes
- 150g green beans
- 8 eggs
- 100g cup mushrooms
- 1 medium red capsicum
- 1 long red chili
- 1 ½ tablespoon vegetable oil
- 1½ tablespoons fish sauce
- 2 tablespoons lime juice

Method:

1. Combine the lemon juice, salmon sauce, 1 teaspoon sweet chili sauce, and the fried grain of your selection in a small bowl; cast aside.

2. In a small mixing cup, whisk together the whites and the additional ½ teaspoon of chili paste; put down.

3. Heat ½ tablespoon oil over a moderate flame in a big heavy sauté bowl.

4. Heat the shallots, spring onions white pieces, and bacon, if using, along with the spring onions.

5. Cook for two minutes with the scallion leaves and the remainder ½ tablespoon of oil.

6. Drop in the beaten egg and heat for thirty minutes without stirring.

7. Put in the grain combination and cook for 1 minute, rotating with a spoon until cooked through.

2.10 Thai Chicken Skewers with Dipping Sauce

Cooking Time: 30 minutes

Serving Size: 6

Ingredients:

- 2 green onions
- Olive oil spray
- 1 lb. chicken breast
- 1 cup cherry tomatoes
- 1 small zucchini

For the Thai Dipping Sauce

- 2/3 cup teriyaki sauce
- 1/3 cup peanut butter creamy
- 3 tablespoon orange juice
- 1 teaspoon cayenne pepper
- 2 garlic cloves

Method:

1. Slice Chicken and veggies into bite-size pieces.
2. After that, string the chicken and vegetables together.
3. With a knife, cover the fillets in the side dish, put them on the rack, sprinkle with olive oil, and then position the rack in the air fryer.
4. Heat for ten minutes at 400°F, basting halfway through.

5. On a tray, organize the skewers.

6. Mix all of the sauce components thoroughly.

7. Put aside around a third of a cup in a separate shallow bowl for dipping.

2.11 Thai Fries

Cooking Time: 17 minutes

Serving Size: 2

Ingredients:

- ½ teaspoon paprika
- ½ teaspoon onion powder
- ½ teaspoon salt
- ½ teaspoon garlic powder
- 2 teaspoons arrowroot starch
- 2 teaspoons olive oil
- 1 sweet potato

Method:

1. Slice the sweet potato and carve it into ¼-inch thick strips.

2. Toss the chips with the arrowroot flour in a large mixing cup.

3. Heat the air fryer to 360 degrees Fahrenheit.

4. Toss the chips in the canola oil to thoroughly coat them, then apply the leftover spice and toss once more.

5. Organize the fries in a thin layer and bake for ten minutes at 360°F.

6. Remove the fried fries from the pan and set them aside.

7. As they will get weaker as they cool, serve them
   warm straight away.

2.12 Thai Squash Soup

Cooking Time: 30 minutes

Serving Size: 8

Ingredients:

- Cinnamon and nutmeg
- ½ cup coconut milk
- ¼ teaspoon black pepper
- ⅛ teaspoon cayenne
- 1 white onion
- ½ teaspoon salt
- 2 cups vegetable stock
- 1 butternut squash
- 1 sprig of fresh sage
- 1 carrot
- 1 apple
- 4 cloves garlic

Method:

1. In an Instant Pot cooking pot, combine vegetables broth, ginger, carrot, apple, butternut, basil, pepper, cinnamon, spice, smoked paprika, cinnamon, and nutmeg. Toss all together.

2. Click "Manual" for ten minutes, then "High Pressure" for another ten minutes.

3. Add the coconut milk and blend well.

4. Puree the soup with an electric mixer until it is fully smooth.

5. If required, sprinkle with more salt, pepper, and
   smoked paprika.

2.13 Bacon & Egg Pad Thai with Peas

Cooking Time: 37 minutes

Serving Size: 4

Ingredients:

For the Sauce

- 1 tablespoon sesame oil
- 1 tablespoon Sriracha
- 2 tablespoons peanut butter
- 5 cloves garlic
- ¼ cup soy sauce
- 2 tablespoons fish sauce
- ¼ cup chicken broth
- ¼ cup rice vinegar
- ¼ cup brown sugar

For the Pad Thai

- 1 cup bean sprouts
- 1 red bell pepper
- 8 oz. rice noodles
- 2 zucchini
- 1 cup matchstick carrots
- ¼ cup green onion
- 1 lb. chicken breast

Method:

1. Mix all of the sauce components in a medium mixing cup.

2. Pour the mixture over the diced meat in the Instant Cooker.

3. On top, arrange the carrots and spring onions.

4. Cook for four minutes on high pressure in a pressure cooker.

5. In the meantime, bring a big pot of water to the stove and prepare the rice noodles.

6. Combine the zucchini, bean sprouts, and red pepper in a mixing dish.

7. Use tongs to gently mix the rice noodles with the steamed vegetables in the Instant Pot.

8. Enable them to heat up for a few minutes.

9. Mix thoroughly with the garnishes of your choosing.

2.14 Thai Style Popcorn

Cooking Time: 1 hour 10 minutes

Serving Size: 8

Ingredients:

- 1 cup bean sprouts
- ½ cup fresh coriander leaves
- 2 medium tomatoes
- 150g green beans
- 1 pack kernels
- 1 long red chili
- 1 ½ tablespoon vegetable oil
- 2 tablespoons lime juice
- 1 ½ tablespoons fish sauce

Method:

1. Preheat the oven to 250 degrees Fahrenheit.
2. Use foil rubbed with olive oil or a synthetic baking sheet to line a cookie sheet.
3. In a big saucepan, heat 1 tablespoon peanut oil.
4. Pan and simmer, frequently shaking, until popcorn is completely popped, around five minutes.
5. Place the popcorn in a big mixing bowl.
6. In a wide pan over medium heat, mix sour cream, ¼ cup sunflower oil, and cane sugar.
7. Stir the brown sugar solution into the popcorn to coat it.

8. Popcorn should be laid out on the baking tray that has been prepared.

9. Allow for cooling and crisping. When serving, combine with coriander.

2.15 Sticky Thai Meatballs

Cooking Time: 30 minutes

Serving Size: 6

Ingredients:

Meatballs

- 1 tablespoon fish sauce
- 2 tablespoon tapioca starch
- 1 tablespoon grated ginger
- 1 tablespoon red curry paste
- 1 ½ lb. ground beef
- 3 garlic cloves
- ¼ cup basil leaves
- ½ onion

Coconut Curry Sauce

- 2 teaspoon turmeric powder
- Lime wedges to serve
- 1 14-oz can coconut milk
- 1 tablespoon fish sauce
- 1 tablespoon grated ginger
- 1 tablespoon red curry paste
- ½ onion diced
- 4 garlic cloves minced
- 1 tablespoon coconut oil

Method:

1. In a large mixing bowl, combine all of the meatball components.

2. Make 30 golf-sized balls out of the dough.

3. Set the Instant Pot to Sauté mode.

4. Pour in the coconut oil. Cook, frequently stirring, for three minutes, or until the onion is translucent.

5. Heat for two minutes, or until onion, rosemary, ginger, and red curry paste are fragrant.

6. After the Instant Pot has been turned off, add the coconut milk, shrimp paste, and turmeric powder.

7. In a separate bowl, combine the meatballs and the sauce.

8. Cook for five minutes on high on the manual setting.

9. Remove the lid and set the Instant Pot to Sauté mode.

10. Cook for 5-10 minutes, or until the sauce has thickened and reduced.

11. Before eating, drizzle with lemon juice and minced basil.

2.16 Thai Congee Recipe

Cooking Time: 1 hour

Serving Size: 6

Ingredients:

- Green onions for garnish
- Salt to taste
- 6 chicken drumsticks
- 1 tablespoon ginger
- 7 cups cold water
- ¾ cup Jasmine rice

Method:

1. In an Instant Pot, mix ginger, 5-6 chicken thighs, and 6.5 - 7 cups ice water.
2. Heat for thirty minutes at high pressure in a pressure cooker.
3. Use the Sauté feature to heat the Instant Pot.
4. Sprinkle with salt after stirring the congee until it reaches the desired consistency and quality.
5. Separate the meat products from the bones with tweezers and a fork.
6. Take the congee from the flame and top it with spring onions.

2.17 Vegetarian Thai Yellow Curry

Cooking Time: 30 minutes

Serving Size: 4

Ingredients:

Curry

- ¼ cup roasted cashews
- 1 medium lemon
- ¼ cup green peas
- 2 ripe mangos
- 1 ½ tablespoon coconut oil
- 1 teaspoon ground turmeric
- 1 red bell pepper
- 1 medium shallot
- ¼ teaspoon sea salt
- 2-3 teaspoon tamari
- 2 tablespoon fresh ginger
- 2 14-ounce coconut milk
- 3 tablespoon coconut sugar
- 2 cloves minced garlic
- 1 cup chopped red cabbage
- 3 tablespoon red curry paste
- 1 Thai red chili

Method:

1. Over medium-high heat, heat a big cast-iron skillet.

2. Add the coconut oil, red onion, carrot, cloves, and peppers once the pan is warmed.

3. Add a pinch of salt and cook, constantly stirring, for three minutes.

4. Stir in the cabbage and red curry spice, and bake for another two minutes.

5. Stir in coconut milk, maple syrup, sea salt, soya sauce, and turmeric.

6. Reduce heat to low and add bell pepper and peas.

7. Heat, stirring periodically, for 5-ten minutes to soften the peppers and peas and incorporate them with curry flavor.

8. After the broth has been well-seasoned and the peppers have lightened, add the mango, cashew nuts, and lime juice and continue to cook for 3-4 minutes.

9. Serve with steamed broccoli and rice or coconut brown rice.

2.18 Thai Green Curry with Homemade Curry Paste

Cooking Time: 30 minutes

Serving Size: 6

Ingredients:

- 2 teaspoon Thai fish sauce
- 3 tablespoon olive oil
- 1 teaspoon ground cumin
- 1 teaspoon black peppercorns
- 8 kaffir lime leaves
- 1 tablespoon coriander seeds
- 4-6 medium green chilies
- 2 lemongrass stalks
- 1 lime
- 2 shallots
- 2 garlic cloves
- Small bunch coriander
- 5cm fresh ginger

Method:

1. Stir fry ingredients. Put all of the food items in a mixing bowl and blitz to a mixture.

2. Use right away or hold in the refrigerator for up to three days in a jar.

Chapter 3: Thai Lunch, Salad, and Soup Recipes

3.1 Thai Red Curry with Chicken

Cooking Time: 30 minutes

Serving Size: 6

Ingredients:

- 4 lime leaves
- 12 Thai basil leaves
- ½ cup onion
- ½ cup bamboo shoots
- 3 tablespoon Thai red curry paste
- 1 cup green bell pepper
- 1 cup carrots
- 14 oz. coconut milk
- 2 teaspoon brown sugar
- 1 tablespoon lime juice
- ¼ cup chicken broth
- 2 tablespoon fish sauce
- 1 lb. boneless chicken breasts

Method:

1. Pick Sauté and cook until the red curry paste and 1/2 can of coconut milk are bubbly.

2. Combine the chicken, the leftover coconut milk, and the chicken broth in a mixing dish.

3. Put the lid and steam for four minutes on a high flame.

4. Add bell pepper, peppers, carrots, green onions, lemongrass, fish sauce, corn syrup, and lemon juice.

5. Press 'Sauté' and cook for 5 minutes, or until veggies are crunchy.

6. Taste and modify seasonings with additional fish sauce, cocoa powder, or lime juice as required.

7. Insert the Thai basil leaves and blend well.

3.2 Thai Panang Curry

Cooking Time: 30 minutes

Serving Size: 6

Ingredients:

- 4 lime leaves
- 15 Thai basil leaves
- 1 cup green beans
- ½ cup onion
- 3 tablespoon Thai curry paste
- 2 tablespoon peanut butter
- 1 cup red bell pepper
- 1 tablespoon brown sugar
- 2 teaspoon lime juice
- 1 teaspoon coriander powder
- 1½ lb. chicken breasts
- 2 tablespoon fish sauce
- 14 oz. coconut milk
- ½ teaspoon cumin powder

Method:

1. Pick sauté and combine ingredients.

2. In the inner cup, combine the Penang curry paste, cilantro, smoked paprika, and half a can of coconut milk.

3. Combine the chicken and the leftover coconut milk in a mixing bowl.

4. Shut the lid and steam for four minutes on a high flame.

5. Stir in the fish sauce, cinnamon, lemon juice, whipped cream, bell pepper, peas, onion, and lime leaves, as well as the bell pepper, veggies, onion, and bay leaves.

6. Pick sauté and cook for five minutes, or until veggies are buttery.

7. Add more fish sauce, black pepper, lemon juice, or peanut butter to taste.

8. Add the Thai basil leaves and mix well.

3.3 Chicken Pad Thai

Cooking Time: 37 minutes

Serving Size: 4

Ingredients:

For the Sauce

- 1 tablespoon sesame oil
- 1 tablespoon Sriracha
- 2 tablespoons peanut butter
- 5 cloves garlic
- ¼ cup soy sauce
- 2 tablespoons fish sauce
- ¼ cup chicken broth
- ¼ cup rice vinegar
- ¼ cup brown sugar

For the Pad Thai

- 1 cup bean sprouts
- 1 red bell pepper
- 8 oz. rice noodles
- 2 zucchini
- 1 cup matchstick carrots
- ¼ cup green onion
- 1 lb. chicken breast

Method:

1. Mix all of the sauce components in a medium mixing cup.

2. Pour the mixture over the diced meat.

3. On top, arrange the carrots and spring onions.

4. Cook for four minutes on high flame.

5. In the meantime, bring a big pot of water to the stove and prepare the rice noodles.

6. Combine the zucchini, bean sprouts, and red pepper in a mixing dish.

7. Use tongs to mix the rice noodles with the steamed vegetable gently.

8. Enable them to heat up for a few minutes.

9. Mix thoroughly with the garnishes of your choosing.

3.4 Rainbow Thai Salad with Mango

Cooking Time: 30 minutes

Serving Size: 4

Ingredients:

For the Dressing

- ¼ teaspoon red chili flakes
- Salt and freshly ground black pepper
- 1 teaspoon sesame oil
- 2 cloves garlic
- ¼ cup creamy peanut butter
- 2 tablespoons lime juice
- 1 tablespoon fresh ginger
- 2 tablespoons soy sauce
- 2 tablespoons honey
- 3 tablespoons rice vinegar

For the Salad

- 1 green onion
- ¼ cup cashews
- ¼ cup cilantro
- 8 fresh mint leaves
- 2 cups kale
- ½ cup carrot
- 1 mango
- 1 ½ cups red cabbage

- ½ cup red bell pepper
- 1 ½ cups Napa cabbage

Method:

1. Whisk along sour cream, garlic powder, soy sauce, sugar, lemon zest, ginger, soy sauce, seasoning, fresh basil, and salt and black pepper to blend in a small pan to make the coating.

2. If the coating is too dense, add a teaspoon of water at a time to smooth it out.

3. Combine the kale, broccoli, red pepper, cabbage, mango, coriander, basil, and onions in a big mixing bowl.

4. Sprinkle the dressing over the salad, toss to blend, and top with cashews.

3.5 Coconut Chicken Curry

Cooking Time: 50 minutes

Serving Size: 5

Ingredients:

- ½ teaspoon ginger powder
- ¼ teaspoon cayenne
- 1 ½ teaspoon garlic powder
- 1 teaspoon salt
- 1½ pounds chicken thighs
- 2 tablespoons Thai red curry paste
- 1 tablespoon sweet chili sauce
- 2 tablespoons peanut butter
- 1 14 ounces can coconut milk

Garnish

- Crushed peanuts
- 1 lime cut into wedges
- A handful of Thai basil

Method:

1. In a 6 quart instant bowl, combine the coconut milk, sour cream, red curry paste, chili sauce, and seasoning.

2. The chicken should then be added to the pot.

3. Cook for five minutes at high flame after locking the cover and shutting the pressure valve.

4. Pressure will naturally be released.

5. Shred the meat into the curry with two forks.

6. If needed, top with Thai oregano and diced peanuts.

3.6 Thai Peanut Noodles

Cooking Time: 25 minutes

Serving Size: 2

Ingredients:

- Juice of 1 lime
- Crushed peanuts
- 8 oz. spaghetti
- 1.5 cups water
- 2 tablespoons oil
- 3 tablespoon peanut butter
- Salt to taste
- 4-5 garlic cloves
- 1.5 tablespoons honey
- 1 tablespoon sriracha
- 2.5 tablespoons soy sauce
- 1.5 tablespoons rice vinegar
- 1-inch ginger minced
- 1 medium red pepper
- 3 stalks green onion
- 2 medium carrots

Method:

1. When the pan is heated, add the oil, followed by the diced ginger and garlic.
2. Sauté for a moment, or until the color of the garlic and ginger begins to change.

3. Toss in the herbs.

4. Push the vegetables to the sides of the pot and add the sesame oil, garlic powder, honey, sriracha, peanut butter, and salts to the middle.

5. Split the pasta in half and transfer it to the pot.

6. Pour in enough water to barely cover the spaghetti.

7. Place the lid on the pot. Heat for four minutes on a high flame.

8. Toss in the reserved green onion leaves, one lemon juice, and coriander.

9. Serve with crushed peanuts on top of the pasta!

3.7 Chopped Thai Salad with Sesame Garlic Dressing

Cooking Time: 25 minutes

Serving Size: 6

Ingredients:

For the Dressing

- 1 tablespoon lemongrass paste
- A squeeze of lime juice
- 2 tablespoons honey
- 1 tablespoon sesame oil
- 2 tablespoons water
- 2 tablespoons vinegar
- 3 cloves garlic
- 3 tablespoons soy sauce
- 1/3 cup canola oil

For the Salad

- 3 green onions
- ¾ cup cashews
- 2 bell peppers
- 1 cup cilantro leaves
- 5–6 cups baby kale
- 3 large carrots
- 16 ounces shelled edamame

Method:

1. In a spice grinder, puree all of the coating components until creamy.

2. Taste and adapt according to your personal preferences.

3. Rinse the stick blender and store it in a dressing container for later use.

4. Simmer the edamame in a pot of water for 3-five minutes to prepare it.

5. Drain the water and set it aside to settle.

6. In a stick blender, spin the cooked edamame five times to have a mashed consistency.

7. Move the cashews to a container and continue the cycle.

8. Drizzle the sauce over the salad, toss gently just a few times, and serve right away.

3.8 Crunchy Thai Salad with Peanut Dressing

Cooking Time: 30 minutes

Serving Size: 4

Ingredients:

Thai Salad

- 1 tablespoon green onions
- ¼ cup peanuts
- ¼ cup cilantro
- 8 mint leaves
- 2 cups kale
- ½ cup carrot
- 1 mango
- 1½ cups red cabbage
- ½ cup red bell pepper
- 1½ cups Napa cabbage

Peanut Dressing

- 1 clove garlic
- 1 tablespoon water
- 1 teaspoon sriracha
- ½ teaspoon ginger
- ⅓ cup peanut butter
- 1 ½ tablespoons soy sauce
- 1 teaspoon sesame oil
- 3 tablespoons honey

- 1 ½ tablespoon rice wine vinegar

- 2 tablespoons lime juice

Method:

1. Thinly slice the kale, broccoli, red pepper, pineapple, mango, coriander, mint, and fresh basil into a big mixing bowl.

2. Put down as you prepare the dressing.

3. Add sour cream, lemon juice, sugar, syrup, sesame oil, soy sauce, tzatziki, spice, garlic, and liquid to a blender and blend until smooth.

4. If the covering needs to be thinned out, add a little water. As required, sprinkle with salt.

5. If there's some leftover dressing, sprinkle it on top.

6. Garnish with sliced peanuts and finely crushed black pepper.

3.9 Thai Stir-Fried Vegetables with Garlic, Ginger, and Lime

Cooking Time: 20 minutes

Serving Size: 6

Ingredients:

- Fresh coriander
- Cashew nuts
- Baby corn
- Sesame oil
- Bamboo shoots
- Water chestnuts
- 1 red capsicum
- 3 cups bok choy
- 6 shiitake mushrooms
- 1 small head of broccoli
- ¼ cup shallots
- 1 fresh chili
- 1 carrot, sliced
- 2 thumb size ginger
- 6 cloves garlic

Stir-Fry Sauce

- ½ teaspoon dry chili flakes
- 2½ teaspoons brown sugar
- 3½ tablespoons lime juice

- 1½ tablespoons soy sauce
- 2½ tablespoons fish sauce
- 400ml coconut milk

Method:

1. In a cup or pan, mix all of the components for the stir fry sauce.
2. To remove the sugar, stir vigorously.
3. In a hot wok, pour in the oil.
4. Combine the shallot, garlic, ginger, and chili in a large mixing bowl.
5. Add the carrots and mushrooms, as well as a quarter of the sauce mixture.
6. ½ of the remaining sauce, tomatoes, bell pepper, and bamboo shoots
7. Insert the bok choy and as well as residual sauce.
8. Wrap up the dish with a generous sprinkling of cashew nuts.

3.10 Beef Thai Red Curry Recipe

Cooking Time: 1 hour 5 minutes

Serving Size: 6

Ingredients:

For the Soup

- 6 ounces snap peas
- Jasmine rice
- ¼ teaspoon red pepper
- 1 tablespoon lime juice
- 2 tablespoons maple syrup
- 2¾ pounds beef chuck roast
- 7 ounces coconut milk
- 2 tablespoons lemongrass paste
- 1 teaspoon salt
- 2 sweet peppers
- 1½ cups chicken stock
- 1 teaspoon pepper
- 1 two-inch ginger
- 1 medium yellow onion
- 4 cloves garlic
- 4 ounces Thai red curry paste
- 2 tablespoons coconut oil

Method:

1. Adjust the stove to a sauté level after seasoning the beef chunks with salt and black pepper.

2. Heat the coconut oil. With a serving dish, extract the meat from the stove.

3. Sauté for four minutes with the minced garlic, garlic, and vegetables.

4. Sauté for 1 minute after adding the red curry paste and tarragon paste.

5. Cook style for thirty minutes with the chicken broth and broiled beef.

6. With a serving dish, take the meat and throw it away.

7. Simmer for four minutes after adding the finely diced sweet peppers.

8. Lime juice, sugar, smashed red pepper, peanut butter, snap peas, and raw meat should all be added at this stage.

9. Switch off the heat after another minute of simmering.

3.11 Thai Peanut Curry

Cooking Time: 10 minutes

Serving Size: 4

Ingredients:

- 3 tablespoon red curry paste
- Few Thai green onions
- 1 tablespoon ginger
- 1 tablespoon garlic
- 1 medium onion
- ½ red bell pepper
- 14 oz. Organic tofu

Ingredients for the Sauce

- Half lemon or lime juice
- ½ teaspoon red pepper flakes
- Salt to taste
- 1teaspoon oil
- 1 tablespoon coconut sugar
- 2 tablespoon sriracha
- 1-½ cup coconut milk
- ¼ cup water
- 1 tablespoon soy sauce
- ¼ cup creamy peanut butter

Rice

- 1 cup of water

- 1 cup basmati rice

Method:

1. Mix coconut milk, whipped cream, sesame oil, barbecue sauce, sugar, and liquid in a medium mixing bowl until smooth.

2. When the skillet is heated, add the oil, diced onions, red pepper, garlic, cloves, and stir to mix.

3. Combine the red curry powder, coconut, and almond sauce in a mixing dish.

4. Toss in the pieces of tofu.

5. Toss in some water and season with salt to taste.

6. Place the trivet on top of the rice with care.

7. Cook for five minutes on a high flame with the lid on.

8. Offer it in a bowl of rice and sliced roasted peanuts on top.

3.12 Vegetable Fried Rice with Cashews

Cooking Time: 30 minutes

Serving Size: 4

Ingredients:

- Steamed rice
- 50g toasted cashew nuts
- 60 ml vegetable stock
- 75g English spinach leaves
- 300g slender eggplants
- 3 ripe tomatoes
- Two tablespoons vegetable oil
- 70g balti curry paste
- 1 onion

Method:

1. Heat a skillet or a deep cooking pot to a high temperature.
2. Swirl in the oil to evenly cover the side.
3. Boil the onions for 3-4 minutes over medium temperature or until translucent.
4. Heat for 1 minute after adding the curry paste, then insert the eggplant and cook over medium heat.
5. Gently throw in the tofu for four minutes or until translucent.
6. Cook for three minutes, or until the tomato is tender, after adding the tomato and stock.

7. Cook, constantly stirring, until the spinach is only wilted.

8. Season with salt and pepper to taste, then serve.

3.13 Thai Chicken Soup

Cooking Time: 30 minutes

Serving Size: 6

Ingredients:

- 1 tablespoon lime zest
- 2 tablespoon cilantro
- 1 can coconut milk
- 2 tablespoon lime juice
- 2 tablespoon sugar
- 4 cups chicken broth
- 4 carrots
- 12 oz. chicken breasts
- 2 tablespoon Thai red curry paste
- 5 oz. shiitake mushrooms
- 1 medium red bell pepper

Method:

1. On a Stove, combine the vegetables, bell pepper, mushrooms, meat, curry paste, butter, and stock.

2. Preheat the pan to high flame and set the timer for four minutes.

3. Mix in the coconut milk after removing the chicken from the oven.

4. Return the shredded chicken to the oven.

5. Cook for an additional minute or until hot on the sauté level.

6. Just before eating, insert the lime zest and juice.

3.14 Thai Mango Chicken

Cooking Time: 35 minutes

Serving Size: 4

Ingredients:

- 1 teaspoon ginger
- 3 garlic cloves
- 1 teaspoon salt
- 1 teaspoon pepper
- 2 ripe mangoes
- 2 limes
- 2 tablespoons turmeric
- 4 large chicken breasts

Method:

1. Cut vegetables.
2. Toss the chicken thighs with the sliced mango in the pan.
3. Over the chicken thighs and mango, add the chicken stock and lemon juice.
4. In the pan, combine the garlic and ginger.
5. Add the turmeric, pepper, and spice to taste.
6. Adjust the pressure on your Stove to the extreme.
7. Toss the meat with the rice after it has been shredded.
8. Serve with pineapple pieces on the side.

3.15 Thai Chicken Noodle Bowls

Cooking Time: 10 minutes

Serving Size: 2

Ingredients:

- ½ red bell pepper
- ½ green bell pepper
- 2 carrot
- 1 cup purple cabbage
- 8 oz. spaghetti noodles
- 4 tablespoon cilantro
- ½ cup peanuts
- 1 stalk green onions

Peanut Sauce

- 3 garlic
- Salt to taste
- ½ fresh lime juice
- 1-inch ginger
- ¼ cup peanut butter
- 2 tablespoon maple syrup
- 2 tablespoon Sriracha
- 2-¼ cup water
- 1 tablespoon vinegar
- 1 tablespoon soy sauce

Method:

1. Combine the peanut butter, cayenne pepper, garlic powder, sugar, sriracha, spice, cloves, pepper, and water in a large mixing bowl.

2. To mix the sauce, whisk it well.

3. Separate the pasta into two groups.

4. Split the pasta in half and transfer it to the pot.

5. In a crisscross pattern, transfer pasta to the inner pot.

6. Put the cover back on.

7. Set the timer to five minutes in the Automatic or Pressure Cook setting.

8. Add the chopped vegetables, toss them together with a tong, and then cover and set aside for five minutes.

9. Squeeze in the lemon juice and serve with green onions and sliced roasted peanuts as a side dish.

3.16 Carrot Soup

Cooking Time: 25 minutes

Serving Size: 6

Ingredients:

- ½ teaspoon ground black pepper
- ¼ cup fresh basil
- ¼ teaspoon red pepper flakes
- 1 teaspoon sea salt
- 1 cup canned coconut milk
- 1 tablespoon fresh lime juice
- 1 tablespoon coconut oil
- 4 cups vegetable broth
- 1 teaspoon honey
- 1 small onion
- 2 garlic cloves
- 1 tablespoon Thai red curry paste
- 1 lb. carrots

Method:

1. Steam the olive oil in the Stove using the Sauté feature.

2. Combine the onion and carrots in a large mixing bowl.

3. Sauté until vegetables are transparent, around 3–5 minutes.

4. Combine the spice and curry paste in a mixing dish.

5. Continue to cook for another minute. Except for three tablespoons of basil, combine the rest of the ingredients.

6. Set the timer to 20 minutes and click the Soup icon.

7. Allow ten minutes for pressure to release after the timer beeps naturally.

8. Using an immersion blender, puree the soup.

9. Serve hot, ladled into bowls, and garnished with ½ teaspoon basil.

3.17 Thai Green Curry with Broccoli Rabe

Cooking Time: 30 minutes

Serving Size: 4

Ingredients:

- ½ cup cilantro
- 2 tablespoon sesame seeds
- 1 bunch broccoli rabe
- 2 cups jasmine rice
- 1 tablespoon olive oil
- 1 bulb fennel
- 3 russet potatoes
- 2 cloves garlic
- 1 8-oz can coconut milk
- 2 tablespoon soy sauce
- 2 chicken breasts
- 2-3 tablespoon green curry paste
- 1 tablespoon ginger

Method:

1. In the pan, combine all ingredients except the vegetable rabe, rice, and garnishes.

2. Cook for an additional minute on high flame.

3. Rice can be cooked on the gas stove or in a pressure cooker in the meantime.

4. Remove lid and let stay for another two minutes after inserting broccoli rabe.

5. Serve the curry with rice and a sprinkle of
   coriander and sesame seeds on it.

3.18 Butternut Squash Soup

Cooking Time: 30 minutes

Serving Size: 8

Ingredients:

- Cinnamon and nutmeg
- ½ cup coconut milk
- ¼ teaspoon black pepper
- ⅛ teaspoon cayenne
- 1 white onion
- ½ teaspoon salt
- 2 cups vegetable stock
- 1 butternut squash
- 1 sprig of fresh sage
- 1 carrot
- 1 apple
- 4 cloves garlic

Method:

1. In a stove cooking pot, combine vegetables broth, ginger, carrot, apple, butternut, basil, pepper, cinnamon, spice, smoked paprika, cinnamon, and nutmeg. Toss all together.

2. Cook on "High flame" for another ten minutes.

3. Add the coconut milk and blend well.

4. Puree the soup with an electric mixer until it is fully smooth.

5. If required, sprinkle with more salt, pepper, and
   smoked paprika.

Chapter 4: Thai Dinner and Desserts Recipes

4.1 Thai Chicken Fried Rice

Cooking Time: 40 minutes

Serving Size: 4

Ingredients:

- ½ teaspoon black pepper
- 3 scallions
- 1 cup white basmati rice
- 1 cup chicken stock
- 4 tablespoons vegetable oil
- 3 garlic cloves
- 2 chicken thighs
- 1 cup onion
- 2 large eggs

Sauce

- 2 tablespoons soy sauce
- 1 teaspoon sugar
- 2 tablespoons oyster sauce

Method:

1. Set the instant pot to the sauté level.
2. Scramble the eggs and transfer them to a dish when they are very soft.

3. Mix in the sliced garlic and onions and cook for another 2-3 minutes before adding the chicken and spreading it out in a single layer.

4. Cook for approximately two minutes.

5. Sauté for about 20 seconds after adding rinsed and soaked rice, then add chicken broth, salt, and pepper.

6. Rice mode should be selected.

7. Cooked eggs, sliced spring onion, oyster sauce, soy sauce, and honey are gently mixed.

8. Before serving, detach the pot, add from the instant pot foundation and set it on a cooling rack for ten minutes.

4.2 Green Thai Coconut Chicken Curry

Cooking Time: 30 minutes

Serving Size: 5

Ingredients:

- ¼ cup coconut
- 2 tablespoon fresh cilantro
- 1 small red chili pepper
- ½ cup bamboo shoots
- ¼ cup lime juice
- 2 teaspoon red pepper
- 1 red bell pepper
- 1 green bell pepper
- 1 tablespoon olive oil
- 1 teaspoon curry powder
- 2 tablespoon coconut sugar
- 1 tablespoon fish sauce
- 2 small zucchini
- 3 tablespoon green Thai curry paste
- 1 14 oz. can of coconut milk
- ½ large sweet onion
- 1.5 lbs. raw chicken breast
- 2 teaspoon ginger

Method:

1. In the Instant Pot, choose the sauté feature.

2. Cover the pot with oils once it's wet.

3. Add the onion and spice now.

4. Cook for 2-3 minutes, stirring periodically.

5. Pour the mixture out of the coconut milk and combine it with the curry paste, garam masala, brown sugar, and fish sauce in a mixing bowl. Add the chicken.

6. Heat for ten minutes on high pressure.

7. Cook, stirring periodically, for 3-5 minutes, or till zucchini and red pepper are tender.

8. In a separate bowl, whisk together the cream part of the coconut milk.

9. Add the lemon juice, bamboo shoots, and any peppers you want to add for extra heat.

10. Serve with rice or cauliflower rice as a side dish.

4.3 Thai Combination Fried Rice

Cooking Time: 11 minutes

Serving Size: 4

Ingredients:

- 2 medium eggs
- Salt & pepper
- 3 tablespoons olive oil
- ½ cup frozen peas
- 2½ cups vegetable broth
- 2 carrots
- 2 cups long-grain rice

Method:

1. In your instant pot, combine rice and vegetable stock.

2. Select "manual" and set the timer for three minutes.

3. Place the rice to the side and select the "sauté" option.

4. Sauté for around a minute with the oil and dried peas before adding it together.

5. In the center of the rice, create a well and pour in the egg mixture.

6. Before switching off the Instant Pot fully, mix the egg into the grain and fry all together for another 1-2 minutes.

7. Sprinkle with salt to taste, if necessary.

4.4 Thai Sweet Sticky Rice with Mango

Cooking Time: 40 minutes

Serving Size: 4

Ingredients:

- 1¼ cups water
- 1 ripe mango
- 1 cup glutinous rice

Coconut Sauce

- 1 leaf knotted
- 2 teaspoon cornstarch
- ¼ cup sugar
- ¼ teaspoon salt
- 1 cup coconut milk

Method:

1. In the inner pot of the Instant Pot, insert 2 cups of water.

2. Wash the sticky rice in water for a few seconds.

3. Fill the rice with 1¼ cup water. Adjust the pressure cooker to high pressure and thirty minutes on the timer.

4. In a frying pan, combine 1 cup coconut milk, salt, spice, and pandan roots.

5. Strip the pandan leaves from the dish.

6. To make a cornflour slurry, combine 2 teaspoons cornstarch with 2 teaspoons water.

7. Pour the remaining ½ cup coconut syrup into a mixture and constantly add over low heat until it hardens significantly.

8. Whereas the sticky rice is still hot, pour half of the coconut sauce over it and stir to combine.

9. Serve with mango pieces or strips.

4.5 Easy Thai Basil Vegetable

Cooking Time: 50 minutes

Serving Size: 6

Ingredients:

- 1 small lime
- 15–20 fresh basil leaves
- 1 tablespoon curry powder
- 2 teaspoon tapioca starch
- 6 chicken thighs
- 1 tablespoon fresh ginger
- 1 teaspoon sea salt
- 1 13.5 oz. can coconut milk
- 1 jalapeno
- 1 tablespoon garlic
- 1 onion
- 2 tablespoon coconut oil

Method:

1. In the Instant Pot, mix all but the olive oil, tapioca, lemon, and herbs.

2. Put the lid on the Instant Pot and set the timer for fifteen minutes at increased Meat configuration speed.

3. Shred the chicken with a fork.

4. After turning off the Instant Pot, whisk in the lemon juice and herb until the leaves are evenly dispersed in the curry.

5. Serve immediately over rice of your choosing.

4.6 Thai Air-Fryer Larb

Cooking Time: 20 minutes

Serving Size: 4

Ingredients:

- ¼ cup red bell pepper
- ¼ cup yellow bell pepper
- 1 lb. lean ground beef
- ½ cup carrots
- 1 cup cabbage
- 1 tablespoon olive oil
- 1 small jalapeno pepper
- 1 small red onion
- 2 tablespoon lime juice
- 2 cloves garlic
- 1 teaspoon fresh ginger
- 1 tablespoon sambal sauce
- 1 teaspoon fish sauce

Method:

1. Preheat the air fryer for five minutes at 350° F.

2. Toss the tomatoes, spices, and lemon juice into the air fryer next, accompanied by the olive oil.

3. Cut ties the ground beef with your hands and spread it on top of the other components.

4. Heat for twenty minutes at 350° F, mixing every
   five minutes or breaking down the ground beef as
   it heats.

5. Serve with rice!

4.7 Thai Custard - Authentic Sangkaya Recipe

Cooking Time: 55 minutes

Serving Size: 8

Ingredients:

- ½ cup of palm sugar
- 1 teaspoon of vanilla extract
- 1 cup of coconut cream
- 4 eggs

Method:

1. The eggs should be whisked together.
2. Combine the coconut milk and coconut sugar in a mixing bowl.
3. In a separate bowl, combine the icing sugar and the water.
4. Fill steam-safe containers with the custard.
5. Fill the coated steamer with the cups.
6. Heat for half an hour or until the custard hits 170 degrees Fahrenheit (75 degrees Celsius).
7. The custard will grow as it firms up.
8. Enable to solidify at room temperature before serving.
9. Serve with rice noodles made with almonds!

4.8 Thai Red Curry Sweet Potato Soup

Cooking Time: 50 minutes

Serving Size: 4

Ingredients:

- 3 teaspoons agave nectar
- ½ cup cilantro
- 1 can coconut milk
- 1 tablespoon fresh lime juice
- 1 large bunch of scallions
- ½ teaspoon kosher salt
- 1 tablespoon tamari
- 1 cup red lentils
- 2 cups vegetable broth
- 5 garlic cloves
- 3 medium plum tomatoes
- 4 tablespoons red curry paste
- 1½ pounds sweet potatoes
- 2 tablespoons ginger

Method:

1. Fill the Instant Pot halfway with vegetable broth.

2. Combine the green onion, cloves, ginger, potatoes, peppers, red curry paste, kidney beans, salt, tamari or soy sauces, and lite coconut milk in a large mixing bowl.

3. Choose a pressure level.

4. Set the pressure cooker to high and the cooking time to ten minutes.

5. Combine the lemon juice, agave or honey, and minced cilantro in a mixing bowl.

6. Taste the broth and season with salt and pepper as needed.

7. To eat, ladle soup into bowls and top with desired garnishes.

8. Hold leftovers refrigerated for up to 4-5 days.

4.9 Coconut Pudding Cake

Cooking Time: 1 hour 5 minutes

Serving Size: 14

Ingredients:

- 1 cup water
- 2 (3 ½ ounce) pudding
- 3 large eggs
- 2 cups cold milk
- 1 (18 ounces) yellow cake mix
- ½ cup vegetable oil
- 1 1/3 cups water

Topping

- 1 cup cold milk
- 1 cup coconut flakes
- 1 (3 ½ ounce) pudding mix

Method:

1. Combine sugar cookie dough, liquid, cooking oil, and eggs in a mixing bowl.

2. Fill an oiled and browned 9 x 13 baking pan halfway with batter.

3. Measure vanilla paste mixes, whipped cream, and water into a big mixing bowl.

4. Just use an electric mixer, blend it until it's completely smooth. Pour the mixture over the cake batter in the pan.

5. Bake for thirty minutes at 350°F or until a spoon inserted in the center comes out dry.

6. Allow thirty minutes for cooling in the pan.

7. Set aside for 1 hour in the fridge. Remove the topping and place it on top.

8. Combine 1 cup whipped cream with 1 cup coconut flavor pudding blend.

9. Press over the cooled cake and top with a sprinkling of coconut.

4.10 Thai Coconut Mango Sticky Rice

Cooking Time: 40 minutes

Serving Size: 4

Ingredients:

- 1¼ cups water
- 1 ripe mango
- 1 cup glutinous rice

Coconut Sauce

- 1 leaf knotted
- 2 teaspoon cornstarch
- ¼ cup sugar
- ¼ teaspoon salt

- 1 cup coconut milk

Method:

1. In the inner pot of the Instant Pot, insert 2 cups of water.

2. Wash the sticky rice in water for a few seconds.

3. Fill the rice with 1¼ cup water. Adjust the pressure cooker to high pressure and thirty minutes on the timer.

4. In a frying pan, combine 1 cup coconut milk, salt, spice, and pandan roots.

5. Strip the pandan leaves from the dish.

6. To make a cornflour slurry, combine 2 teaspoons cornstarch with 2 teaspoons water.

7. Pour the remaining ½ cup coconut syrup into a mixture and constantly add over low heat until it hardens significantly.

8. Whereas the sticky rice is still hot, pour half of the coconut sauce over it and stir to combine.

9. Serve with mango pieces or strips.

4.11 Thai Stir-Fried Mixed Vegetables Recipe

Cooking Time: 40 minutes

Serving Size: 4

Ingredients:

- Thai chilies
- 1 teaspoon sugar
- 5 shiitake mushrooms
- 5 cloves garlic
- 3 stalks Chinese broccoli
- 10 sugar snap peas
- 2 tablespoon oyster sauce
- ¼ head cauliflower
- 3 cups cabbage
- 2 teaspoon soy sauce
- 1 tablespoon water
- ½ cup carrots
- 2 teaspoon golden mountain sauce

Method:

1. Combine oyster sauce, sesame oil, golden mountains seasoning, and water in a small cup.

2. Combine the carrot and cabbage in a mixing dish.

3. Later, add the cabbage, snap beans, gai lan roots, and mushroom.

4. Switch the medium heat in a skillet, or a big sauté pan, insert a little vegetable oil, onions, bell peppers, and sauté.

5. Toss in the carrots and cauliflower for around two minutes over medium heat.

6. Insert bowl 2 of veggies.

7. Toss until the veggies are almost completed to your taste.

8. Add gai lan leaf, toss just until softened.

4.12 Vegetarian Pad Thai with Spicy Sauce

Cooking Time: 25 minutes

Serving Size: 2

Ingredients:

For The Sauce

- 1 tablespoon honey
- 1-3 teaspoons chili garlic sauce
- 1½ tablespoons rice vinegar
- 1 tablespoon soy sauce
- 2 tablespoons fish sauce

For the Vegetarian Pad Thai

- ¼ cup fresh cilantro
- Lime wedges for serving
- 2 large green onions
- ¼ cup peanuts
- 1 cup carrots
- ½ cup shelled edamame
- 2 large eggs
- 1 cup bean sprouts
- 2 medium zucchini
- 2 cloves garlic
- 1 teaspoon olive oil

Method:

1. In a shallow saucepan, stir together all the sauce components.

2. Slice the zucchini into zoodles using a spiralizer.

3. In a large skillet over medium heat or broiler, heat one teaspoon of butter over medium-low heat.

4. After the garlic has been added, smash the eggs into the pan.

5. Break the yolk apart like a spoon and simmer for thirty seconds or until it just starts to settle.

6. Stir in the pasta and sauce to combine.

7. Add the green beans, broccoli, edamame, and sliced spring onions and bake till the bean sprouts are crisp-tender, about five minutes.

8. Toss in the coriander and nuts.

4.13 Thai Air-Fryer Satay Skewers with Peanut Sauce

Cooking Time: 4 hours

Serving Size: 10

Ingredients:

- Salt and black pepper
- 2 ½ pounds chicken thighs
- ½ teaspoon cumin
- ½ teaspoon coriander
- ¼ cup coconut milk
- 2 teaspoons curry powder
- 1 ½ teaspoons turmeric
- 3 tablespoons coconut amino
- 1 tablespoon fish sauce
- 3 cloves garlic
- 1 tablespoon ginger

Dipping Sauce

- 5 cups hot cooked rice
- ½ bunch cilantro sprigs
- 1 teaspoon cayenne pepper
- 2 tablespoons raw cashews
- ½ cup teriyaki sauce
- 3 tablespoons orange juice

- 2 cloves garlic

- ⅓ cup cashew butter

Method:

1. In a quart resealable container, add coconut amino, turmeric, salt, coconut milk, fish sauce, cumin, garlic, coriander, ginger, curry powder, and seasoning.

2. Toss in the chicken bits.

3. Put it in the fridge for at least three hours before serving.

4. In a shallow pan, add the orange juice, cashew butter, teriyaki sauce, garlic, and smoked paprika.

5. Refrigerate before ready to eat, tightly sealed.

6. Preheat the oven to 400 degrees Fahrenheit.

7. Thread chicken parts onto each skewer and put them on the skewer accessory shelf.

8. Air fried for ten minutes with the rack in the air fryer container.

9. On each of the sauces, scatter sliced cashews.

10. Serve the fillets with the dipping sauce on top of hot boiled rice.

4.14 Rainbow Vegetarian Pad Thai with Crispy Noodles

Cooking Time: 30 minutes

Serving Size: 4

Ingredients:

Noodles

- 1 carrot
- 1 tablespoon sesame oil
- 1 yellow capsicum
- 1 brown onion
- 1 green zucchini
- 1 red capsicum
- 250g Thai style rice noodles

Sauce

- 1 teaspoon fish sauce
- 1 teaspoon sriracha chili sauce
- 1 tablespoon rice vinegar
- 1 tablespoon maple syrup
- 3 tablespoon soy sauce

Garnish

- 1 packet fried noodles
- Juice of 1 lime
- 3 green onions

Method:

1. Prepare the noodles as directed on the package.

2. To make the sauce, mix all of the components in a mixing bowl.

3. Add the soy sauce and onions to the skillet and stir fry for two minutes, then add the vegetables and capsicums and stir fry for another two minutes.

4. Finally, mix in the zucchini for just one minute.

5. Place the cooked noodles in the skillet and pour the sauce over them.

6. Return the veggies to the skillet. Merge the noodles with the sauce.

7. Remove from heat and garnish with spring onions, lemon juice, and fried noodles.

8. Combine all ingredients and serve right away.

4.15 Pandan Jelly Dessert Recipe

Cooking Time: 5 minutes

Serving Size: 2

Ingredients:

- ½ cup coconut milk
- 3 tablespoon coconut condensed milk
- 2 teaspoon Japanese agar
- 3 teaspoon sugar
- 1 tablespoon coffee granules
- 2 cups water

Method:

1. In a shallow dish, bring two cups of water to the stove.
2. Reduce to low heat and stir in the agar, coffee crystals, and sucrose.
3. Take the pan off the heat and place it in a shallow bowl.
4. Enable for 5-8 minutes of cooking time or until it reaches room temperature.
5. Create the soft milk by whisking together the vaporized coconut milk and condensed milk, then chilling the mixture.
6. Break the coffee jelly into pieces within the dish with a paring blade.
7. Pour the warm milk and over espresso cubes in the bowls.

4.16 Thai Chicken Wings

Cooking Time: 20 minutes

Serving Size: 4

Ingredients:

- 4 pounds chicken wings

Sauce

- 1 teaspoon ginger
- 1 teaspoon red pepper flakes
- 1/3 cup soy sauce
- 6 cloves garlic
- ½ cup clover honey

Method:

1. In your Pressure Cooker frying pan, add the wings.

2. Combine the sauce components in a mixing bowl and pour over the chicken wings.

3. Heat for four minutes on high pressure.

4. Take the wings from the Slow Cooker with tweezers and put them in the Air Fryer Basket.

5. Heat for ten minutes at 400 degrees Fahrenheit.

6. In the meantime, switch the Pressure Cooker to Sauté and continue to mix the sauce until it thickens.

7. When the wings are fried, dip them in the sauce and serve, or place them back in the Air Fryer to caramelize.

8. Serve with sliced shallots as a garnish.

4.17 Air Fryer Sweet Chili Salmon

Cooking Time: 30 minutes

Serving Size: 4

Ingredients:

- Green onions
- Sesame seeds
- 2 tablespoons soy sauce
- ½ teaspoon pepper
- ½ cup sweet chili sauce
- 4 salmon fillets

Method:

1. Erase any stray bones from the fish fillets by patting them dry with a clean cloth.
2. To satisfy, sprinkle with seasoning.
3. Combine hot chili sauce and sesame oil in a mixing dish.
4. Refrigerate for thirty minutes after marinating.
5. Heat for seven to eight minutes in a preheated 400 F air fryer, based on size.
6. Take from the air fryer and, if needed, cover with finely chopped onions and pumpkin seeds.

4.18 Thai Noodle Bowl with Air Fried Tofu and Peanut Sauce

Cooking Time: 30 minutes

Serving Size: 4

Ingredients:

For the Tofu

- Pinch of dried chili flakes
- 1 tablespoon oil
- ½ teaspoon onion powder
- ¼ teaspoon ground ginger
- 300g firm tofu
- ½ teaspoon ground coriander
- ½ teaspoon garlic powder
- 1 tablespoon cornflour

For the Dressing

- ½ teaspoon grated ginger
- Sriracha chili sauce to taste
- 1 teaspoon sesame oil
- 1 teaspoon minced garlic
- Two tablespoon peanut butter
- Juice of ½ lime
- 2 teaspoon maple syrup
- 2 tablespoon soy sauce

For the Thai Noodle Salad

* 2 carrots spiralizer

* 1 red bell pepper

* ¼ of a red cabbage

* 100g thick rice noodles

Method:

1. Combine the corn flour and seasoning in a shallow cup.

2. Mix the tofu pieces softly in the spice mixture after chopping it.

3. Heat for ten minutes in the air fryer box with one tablespoon oil, then switch and cook for another ten minutes until it is fluffy.

4. Start preparing the seasoning and noodle salads in the meantime.

5. To make the dressing, mix all of the components until creamy.

6. To make the salad, soak the rice noodles in hot water until they are tender.

7. Use a spiralizer to slice all the veggies into long skinny matchsticks.

8. Toss the veggies and pasta with the dressing and serve on individual plates.

9. To eat, finish with tofu and any desired seasonings.

Chapter 5: Most Famous Thai Dishes

5.1 Thai Pork and Lime Risotto

Cooking Time: 30 minutes

Serving Size: 4

Ingredients:

- 2 tablespoons basil
- 1 cup spinach leaves
- ½ teaspoon kosher salt
- Zest and juice of 1 lime
- 2 tablespoons rice vinegar
- 1 tablespoon honey
- ½ cup coconut milk
- ½ cup Arborio rice
- 1 cup chicken broth
- 1 tablespoon green curry paste
- 1 tablespoon coconut oil
- ½ cup yellow onion
- 1 pound pork tenderloin
- 1 tablespoon green curry paste
- Salt and pepper
- 2 tablespoons coconut milk

Method:

1. Put the diced pork in a large bowl or a gallon sealable plastic jar.

2. Stir in the coconut milk, yellow curry spice, salt, and pepper until the meat is thoroughly coated.

3. Fill the stovetop pot with oil.

4. To get some color on the meat and wake up the curry powder, insert the pork and vegetables and sauté for 2-3 minutes. Fill the pot with rice.

5. Scrape any remaining ingredients from the bottom of the container and add chicken broth.

6. ½ cup coconut milk, one tablespoon Thai curry paste, mirin, sugar, salt, and one lemon juice are mixed.

7. Cook for five minutes on high pressure.

8. Choose sauté and add ½ cup coconut milk, stirring for two minutes.

9. Serve right away with a squeeze of lemon juice and a sprig of broken basil.

5.2 Thai Coconut Curry Meatballs

Cooking Time: 30 minutes

Serving Size: 6

Ingredients:

Meatballs

- 1 tablespoon fish sauce
- 2 tablespoon tapioca starch
- 1 tablespoon grated ginger
- 1 tablespoon red curry paste
- 1½ lb. ground beef
- 3 garlic cloves
- ¼ cup basil leaves
- ½ onion

Coconut Curry Sauce

- 2 teaspoon turmeric powder
- Lime wedges to serve
- 1 14-oz can coconut milk
- 1 tablespoon fish sauce
- 1 tablespoon grated ginger
- 1 tablespoon red curry paste
- ½ onion diced
- 4 garlic cloves minced
- 1 tablespoon coconut oil

Method:

1. In a large mixing bowl, combine all of the meatball components.

2. Make 30 golf-sized balls out of the dough.

3. Set the Instant Pot to Sauté mode.

4. Pour in the coconut oil. Cook, frequently stirring, for three minutes, or until the onion is translucent.

5. Heat for two minutes, or until onion, rosemary, ginger, and red curry paste are fragrant.

6. After the Instant Pot has been turned off, add the coconut milk, shrimp paste, and turmeric powder.

7. In a separate bowl, combine the meatballs and the sauce.

8. Cook for five minutes on high on the manual setting.

9. Remove the lid and set the Instant Pot to Sauté mode.

10. Cook for 5-10 minutes, or until the sauce has thickened and reduced.

11. Before eating, drizzle with lemon juice and minced basil.

5.3 Easy Vegetable Stir Fry with Creamy Peanut Sauce

Cooking Time: 25 minutes

Serving Size: 4

Ingredients:

- 3 carrots
- 3 cups Thai basil
- 1 bell pepper
- 2 cups snap peas
- 1 cup uncooked rice
- 2 tablespoon coconut oil
- 1 head broccoli
- 3 large garlic cloves

For the Sauce

- ½ teaspoon sesame oil
- 1 tablespoon coconut sugar
- 1 tablespoon fish sauce
- 2 tablespoon rice vinegar
- 2 tablespoon tamari

Method:

1. Cook rice according to package directions and set aside.

2. Mix all seasoning ingredients in a small bowl and set aside.

3. Melt the coconut oil in a large saucepan over medium heat.

4. Add garlic and simmer for one moment.

5. It should turn a golden brown color but not burn. Keep a close eye on things.

6. Broccoli, red pepper, peas, and vegetables are all good additions.

7. Enable 3 minutes for the vegetables to steam.

8. Stir in the basil and cook for another 1-2 minutes, or until the basil has wilted.

5.4 Ramen Pad Thai

Cooking Time: 12 minutes

Serving Size: 4

Ingredients:

- 1 tablespoon cornstarch
- 1 tablespoon tamari
- 1 tablespoon oil
- 1 teaspoon turmeric
- 2 cakes of ramen noodles
- 1 tablespoon garlic
- 4 lime wedges
- 1 teaspoon ginger
- 8 oz. crispy tofu
- 2 cups zucchini slices
- 1 cup scallions
- 8-10 fresh cilantro sprigs
- 1 cup onion sliced
- ½ cup bell peppers
- 10 oz. broth
- 1 tablespoon sesame seeds
- 2 cups broccoli florets
- 1 can coconut milk
- 2 tablespoon chili garlic oil
- 2 tablespoon tamari

- 3 tablespoon Thai red curry paste

Method:

1. Add the oil to the cooking pot using the sauté feature.

2. Add the sliced garlic and cook until the aroma fills the space.

3. Toss in the vegetables.

4. After that, add the Thai Curry paste, coconut milk, and liquid or broth.

5. Combine all of the components in a large mixing bowl and combine well.

6. Place the raw Ramen noodles Cakes on top.

7. Put the lid and steam for 0 minutes under heat.

8. In a large mixing bowl, thoroughly blend the noodles.

9. Toss in the crispy or clean tofu, along with coriander, green onions, roasted white and black sesame seeds, and a dash of sriracha if desired.

5.5 Thai Chicken Stir Fry

Cooking Time: 22 minutes

Serving Size: 5

Ingredients:

Sauce

- 1 cup Thai basil leaves
- 1½ lb. lean ground chicken
- 2 tablespoon grapeseed oil
- 1 tablespoon garlic
- 1 large onion
- 2 red bell pepper
- 2 tablespoon lime juice
- 2 tablespoon soy sauce
- 1 tablespoon agave
- 2 tablespoon sriracha sauce
- 2 tablespoon fish sauce

Method:

1. Combine the lemon juice, shrimp paste, Sriracha Sauce, sesame oil, and Agave nectar in a small cup.

2. Set aside your onions and bell pepper slices that have been thinly cut.

3. Transfer the oil to the Instant Pot and set it to sauté.

4. Heat for 1-2 minutes, or just until moist, after adding the garlic.

5. Cook for four minutes, constantly stirring, in the instant pot with the onion and red pepper pieces.

6. In the Instant Pot, add the remaining teaspoon of oil.

7. Cook for 3-four minutes after adding the ground chicken.

8. Return the veggies to the Instant Pot, along with the sauce, and whisk to mix.

9. At manual-high speed, set the timer for two minutes.

10. Stir in the diced Thai basil until everything is well combined.

5.6 Thai Curry Lentils

Cooking Time: 40 minutes

Serving Size: 6

Ingredients:

- Cilantro for garnishing
- Rice for serving
- ¾ cup coconut milk
- 2 tablespoons butter
- One 14-ounce can of tomato sauce
- 1 teaspoon coarse salt
- 1-inch knob of ginger
- 2 cups water
- 1½ cups brown lentils
- ½ teaspoon turmeric
- 2 cloves garlic
- ½ large onion
- 1 teaspoon garam masala
- 1 teaspoon curry powder
- 1 tablespoon sugar
- 2 tablespoons red curry

Method:

1. In the Instant Pot, combine all of the components.
2. Cook for fifteen minutes on high pressure.

3. Allow for another ten minutes of natural pressure
   release.

4. Combine the coconut milk and butter in a mixing
   dish.

5. Season with salt and pepper to taste.

6. Serve with rice and cilantro on top.

5.7 Thai Basil Chicken Curry with Coconut Milk

Cooking Time: 50 minutes

Serving Size: 6

Ingredients:

- 1 small lime
- 15–20 fresh basil leaves
- 1 tablespoon curry powder
- 2 teaspoon tapioca starch
- 6 chicken thighs
- 1 tablespoon fresh ginger
- 1 teaspoon sea salt
- 1 13.5 oz. can coconut milk
- 1 jalapeno
- 1 tablespoon garlic
- 1 onion
- 2 tablespoon coconut oil

Method:

1. In the Instant Pot, mix all but the olive oil, tapioca, lemon, and herbs.

2. Put the lid on the Instant Pot and set the timer for fifteen minutes at increased Meat configuration speed.

3. Shred the chicken with a fork.

4. After turning off the Instant Pot, whisk in the lemon juice and herb until the leaves are evenly dispersed in the curry.

5. Serve immediately over rice of your choosing.

5.8 Thai Fish Cakes

Cooking Time: 20 minutes

Serving Size: 2

Ingredients:

- ¼ teaspoon pepper
- 2 lime wedges
- Cooking spray
- 1 large egg
- ⅛ teaspoon salt
- 10 ounces white fish
- 2 tablespoons Thai sweet chili sauce
- 2 tablespoons canola mayonnaise
- 3 tablespoons cilantro
- ⅔ cup breadcrumbs

Method:

1. Oil the air fryer container with melted butter.
2. In a medium mixing dish, add the tuna, panko, cilantro, chili sauce, mayo, egg, pepper, and seasoning.
3. Create four 3-inch-diameter cakes out of the combination.
4. Cover the cakes in the baking dish and put them in the basket that has been packed.
5. Heat at 400 degrees F for ten minutes, or until the cakes are golden brown and the core temperature exceeds 140 degrees F.

6. Offer lemon wedges on edge.

5.9 Cauliflower with Sweet Chili Sauce

Cooking Time: 40 minutes

Serving Size: 4

Ingredients:

- ¼ cup sweet chili sauce
- Salt and pepper to taste
- ½ tablespoon avocado oil
- 4 cups cauliflower florets

Method:

1. Mix the cauliflower with the sunflower oil, spice, and seasoning in a large mixing cup.

2. Put the cauliflower in the air fryer container and cook for fifteen minutes at 390 degrees, or till it has ripened and begun to soften.

3. Toss the cabbage with the hot chili sauce to mix.

4. Turn down the heat to 360 degrees and simmer for another five to ten minutes till the cauliflower is buttery.

5.10 Thai Chicken Thighs

Cooking Time: 30 minutes

Serving Size: 4

Ingredients:

- Sea salt

- Black pepper to taste
- 2 teaspoons ginger
- 1 teaspoon garlic powder
- 2 tablespoons sesame oil
- 2 tablespoons honey
- 1½ tablespoons sriracha sauce
- ¼ cup coconut amino
- 2 tablespoons lime juice
- 2/3 cup chicken broth
- ¼ cup peanut butter
- 2 pounds chicken thighs

Method:

1. Adjust the Instant Pot's "Sauté" mode to maximum and add sesame oil.

2. Scoop up the excess liquid from the bottom of the hot container of chicken stock.

3. Stir in the peanut butter until it is fully melted in the hot liquid.

4. Combine the coconut amino acids, lemon juice, sugar, Sriracha sauce, spice, and garlic powder in a mixing bowl.

5. Season with salt and chili flakes and stir to blend.

6. Position the golden brown chicken breasts on top of the metal rack in the Instant Pot.

7. Change the cooking time to ten minutes after turning the "Manual" mode to high.

8. Remove the chicken from the pan and put it on a serving tray.

5.11 Vegetarian Thai Noodles

Cooking Time: 15 minutes

Serving Size: 4

Ingredients:

For the Pad Thai

- ½ cup peanuts
- ½ cup fresh herbs
- 2 tablespoons oil
- 1 egg, beaten
- 4 ounces brown rice noodles
- Half a yellow onion
- 2 carrots
- 1 red pepper
- 1 zucchini

For the Sauce

- 1 tablespoon soy sauce
- 1 teaspoon chili paste
- 3 tablespoons vegetable broth
- 2 tablespoons white vinegar
- 3 tablespoons brown sugar
- 3 tablespoons fish sauce

Method:

1. To soak the undercooked noodles, place them in a bowl of ice water.

2. In a pan, mix the sauce ingredients and shake well.

3. Over medium-high pressure, heat a tablespoon of oil.

4. Stir in the vegetables and cook for a few minutes.

5. Add a further tablespoon of oil to a pan.

6. Add the pasta to the hot pan and stir fry for just a moment, using tweezers to toss.

7. Mix in the liquid for another couple of minutes, just until the sauce begins to thicken and adhere to the noodles.

8. With both the tongs, flip it around. The egg combination will cling to the noodles, causing them to become sticky.

9. Remove from heat after adding the veggies and tossing them together.

5.12 Thai Satay Stir-Fry

Cooking Time: 10 minutes

Serving Size: 4

Ingredients:

- Handful basil leaves
- 25g roasted peanuts
- Thumb-sized root ginger
- 300g pack stir-fry vegetable
- 300g pack noodle
- 1 tablespoon oil
- 3 tablespoon sweet chili sauce
- 2 tablespoon soy sauce
- 3 tablespoon peanut butter

Method:

1. To form a delicious satay sauce, combine the peanut butter, chili sauce, water, and sesame oil.

2. Place the pasta in a bowl and cover it with boiling water.

3. To detach, softly stir, then wash completely.

4. In a skillet, heat the oil, then whisk the herb and the tougher vegetables.

5. Stir in the pasta and the remaining vegetables for 1-2 minutes over medium temperature or until the veggies are just fried.

6. Place the vegetables on one side of the pan and the bean paste on the other.

7. Bring the water to a boil. To serve, combine the sauce with the stir-fry, then top with spring onions and peanuts.

5.13 Vegetarian Pad See Ew with Tofu and Chinese Eggplant

Cooking Time: 30 minutes

Serving Size: 4

Ingredients:

- 12 oz. broccoli
- 2 large eggs, beaten
- 2 cloves garlic
- 1 tablespoon water
- 3 tablespoons canola oil
- ⅓ cup shallot
- 2 tablespoons dark soy sauce
- 16 oz. extra firm tofu
- 1 lb. rice noodle
- 1 tablespoon light brown sugar
- 1 teaspoon Thai chili powder
- 3 tablespoons oyster sauce

Method:

1. Mix the sesame oil, vegan oyster sauce, coconut milk, and chili powder in a small cup.

2. Drizzle 2 teaspoons of the sauce over the tofu in a medium dish.

3. In a wide nonstick skillet, heat two tablespoons of oil, circling the pot to coat it.

4. In the same pan, add the rest tablespoon of olive oil.

5. Heat until the shallots are soft and golden brown in the pan.

6. Heat for thirty seconds, or until the garlic and water are fragrant.

7. Heat, sometimes tossing, until the Chinese broccoli is tender.

8. Toss in the stored rice noodles, tofu, and sauces until all is well combined.

9. Toss the eggs with the rest of the ingredients to combine them.

5.14 Thai Chicken Drumsticks

Cooking Time: 45 minutes

Serving Size: 6

Ingredients:

- 1 slice ginger
- 1 tablespoon honey
- 3 garlic cloves
- 2 stalks green onion
- 1 tablespoon peanut oil
- 10 Chinese red chili
- 10 chicken drumsticks

General Tso Sauce

- ¼ cup sugar
- 1 teaspoon sesame oil
- 2 tablespoons Shaoxing wine
- 2 tablespoons black vinegar
- ¼ cup dark soy sauce

Thickener

- 2 tablespoons cold water
- 2 tablespoons cornstarch

Serve

- Hoisin sauce
- 20 pieces lettuce

Method:

1. Preheat the pressure cooker. Pour 1 tablespoon canola oil into the pressure cooker as it's heating up.

2. In a pressure cooker, combine ten dried Chinese red chilies, diced garlic, white stuff of bell peppers, minced ginger, then start releasing their fragrance.

3. Cook for about three minutes.

4. In an Instant Pot, combine the General Tso Sauce and the chicken.

5. Close the lid and heat for 12 minutes at increased speed.

6. In a big mixing bowl, position the chicken.

7. Drop the Chinese red chili from the recipe.

8. Take the sauce right back to a boil in your slow cooker.

9. Place the shredded chicken on top of the lettuce.

10. Serve with finely chopped cabbage as a garnish.

5.15 Healthy Chicken Pad Thai

Cooking Time: 37 minutes

Serving Size: 4

Ingredients:

For the Sauce

- 1 tablespoon sesame oil
- 1 tablespoon Sriracha
- 2 tablespoons peanut butter
- 5 cloves garlic
- ¼ cup soy sauce
- 2 tablespoons fish sauce
- ¼ cup chicken broth
- ¼ cup rice vinegar
- ¼ cup brown sugar

For the Pad Thai

- 1 cup bean sprouts
- 1 red bell pepper
- 8 oz. rice noodles
- 2 zucchini
- 1 cup matchstick carrots
- ¼ cup green onion
- 1 lb. chicken breast

Method:

1. Mix all of the sauce components in a medium mixing cup.

2. Pour the mixture over the diced meat in the Instant Cooker.

3. On top, arrange the carrots and spring onions.

4. Cook for four minutes on high pressure in a pressure cooker.

5. In the meantime, bring a big pot of water to the stove and prepare the rice noodles.

6. Combine the zucchini, bean sprouts, and red pepper in a mixing dish.

7. Use tongs to gently mix the rice noodles with the steamed vegetables in the Instant Pot.

8. Enable them to heat up for a few minutes.

9. Mix thoroughly with the garnishes of your choosing.

5.16 Vegetarian Pad Thai with Zoodles

Cooking Time: 25 minutes

Serving Size: 2

Ingredients:

For The Sauce

- 1 tablespoon honey
- 1-3 teaspoons chili garlic sauce
- 1½ tablespoons rice vinegar
- 1 tablespoon soy sauce
- 2 tablespoons fish sauce

For the Vegetarian Pad Thai

- ¼ cup fresh cilantro
- Lime wedges for serving
- 2 large green onions
- ¼ cup peanuts
- 1 cup carrots
- ½ cup shelled edamame
- 2 large eggs
- 1 cup bean sprouts
- 2 medium zucchini
- 2 cloves garlic
- 1 teaspoon olive oil

Method:

1. In a shallow saucepan, stir together all the sauce components.

2. Slice the zucchini into zoodles using a spiralizer.

3. In a large skillet over medium heat or broiler, heat one teaspoon of butter over medium-low heat.

4. After the garlic has been added, smash the eggs into the pan.

5. Break the yolk apart like a spoon and simmer for thirty seconds or until it just starts to settle.

6. Stir in the pasta and sauce to combine.

7. Add the green beans, broccoli, edamame, and sliced spring onions and bake till the bean sprouts are crisp-tender, about five minutes.

8. Toss in the coriander and nuts.

Conclusion

Thai cuisine is well-known around the world. The core philosophy behind each food, either chili-hot or compared blends, is cohesion. Thai cuisine is a cohesive fusion of centuries-old East and West traditions into something distinctly Thai. Thai cuisine's distinguishing features. A typical Thai meal consists of a variety of dishes that friends and family share. A number of dishes, including sauces, vegetables, stir-fried foods, grilled or cooked meat or fish, and cuisines, are commonly ordered in a cafe. The dishes are served as a group rather than as separate courses. Food is available with a fork and knife, and each food is eaten one at a time with rice. Unprocessed ingredients added sugar or products, and large quantities of fruit and legumes are all part of traditional Thai cuisine. The only way of learning about Thai cuisine is to try it. Read the Thai cookbook and enjoy yourself while tasting everything Thailand has to offer.